BROOKE L. GARDNER

Tea Stains & Cigarettes

First edition

ISBN: 979-8-41-795867-0

Cover art by Brooke L. Gardner

This book was professionally typeset on Reedsy.
Find out more at reedsy.com

For my little brother, Gage, who was too young to know that it gets better

I don't think all writers are sad. I think it's the other way around—all sad people write.

— Lang Leav

Contents

IV   a poet's heartbreak

V   a poet's recovery

Preface

Content Warning: The poems in Tea Stains & Cigarettes contain material relating to, but not limited to: abuse, addiction, blood, body image, death (including children), gore, grief, eating disorders, mental illness, self-harm, sexual assault, suicide, suicidal ideology, trauma, and violence. Reading about these subjects is difficult, unnerving, and depressing. My purpose in writing poetry on these topics is to spread awareness of these issues and to offer guidance to those who would benefit from someone who has experienced similar trauma.

You are not alone.

For as long as I can remember, I have always wished to be a published author. My passion for writing goes back to when I was in elementary school, handwriting stories on torn-up notebook paper. I wrote of superhero sisters and magical beasts, but I wanted to write more realism as I grew older. In middle school, I fell in love with poetry in my first English class with my teacher Mr. Jones. In sixth grade, we covered a poetry unit and discussed the poems of Edgar Allan Poe and Langston Hughes. Since then, poetry has been my biggest passion in life.

I started writing poetry as a form of coping against my mental disorders. It has helped me explain my feelings of anxiety and depression through a creative outlet. I struggled with self-harm, and writing poetry has allowed me to get my emotions out safely and proactively. I was diagnosed with severe anxiety and depression when I was 13 years old, just a child in middle school. In the following years, I attended many therapy sessions and wrote numerous poems about my mental hardships.

I began writing poetry about my unique upbringing as a form of autobiographical poetry. When I was very young, my birth mother neglected me due to her excessive drug use, leaving my maternal grandmother to step in. Many of my poems reflect life during my childhood living with my birth mother and transitioning into a new household. This confusing time inspired me to write my poem, "southern hospitality," which lists memories of mine from the time of my old house. This poem is similar to another of my list poems, "weathered roots," which follows the same formatting and discusses similar subject matter from these memories.

The majority of my poems have melancholic tones. I write directly from the heart when I am most inspired. Negative emotions trigger my inspiration the most, resulting in my poetry having depressing moods. Positive, happier poems do not hold my interest—and they often make me envious of the speaker—so I write more solemn poetry than happy poetry. Realism is much more interesting, in my opinion. This collection of poems is similar to an autobiography in that I guide the reader (you) through my childhood to my current place in the world through my struggles and successes. I hope that one day, people will find comfort in knowing they are not alone with the demons of mental health problems.

I

a poet's origin

in the crisp autumn
a silent plum babe is born
choking on her cord
practicing for her future
–b.l.g.

southern hospitality

i remember steaming tea boiling over
   screeching and sizzling

i remember tobacco-stained
   brown walls discolored for eternity

i remember the smell of malt and wheat
   infiltrating my nostrils and
   assaulting my nasal cavity

i remember sugar-coated counter tops
   leftover from sweetening the tea

i remember sticky fly traps
   hanging in the corners of the dingy walls

i remember the tall grasses in the backyard
   hiding the garden snakes and pestering insects

i remember thunderous screaming and crying
   glass shattering on the kitchen tiles

i remember peeling the paint off the walls
    and the leather off the couch, simple satisfaction

i remember tossing beer bottles at the old,
    abandoned house next door,
    hiding glass-cut fingertips with band-aids

i remember having mountain dew and
    slim jims for lunch, a well-balanced diet

i remember the old house in the ditch,
    before the adoption paperwork and courtroom riots

  -b.l.g.

sugar-coated

i am sorry
   that my mind
   does not taste
   sweet enough
   for you

i am sorry
   that my thoughts
   are not dipped in
   cream and honey
   for you

i am sorry
   that my brain
   is not drizzled in
   chocolate and caramel
   for you

i am sorry
   that my story
   is not coated in
   sugar and syrup

for you

i am sorry
   that my life
   is not topped with
   cherries and sprinkles
   for you

i am sorry
   that my truth
   tastes of
   sour milk and
   spoiled eggs

-b.l.g.

shoes

from my twisted laces
    to my worn-out soles,
    from my dirty leather
    to my tattered holes,

from my rusty eyelets
    to my wrinkled tongue,
    from my ripped heels
    to my toes overhung,

from my swollen ankles
    to my too-sore legs
    from my sweaty socks
    to my stripped threads

from achy feet, blistered skin
    to running all night
    from my demons within,
    to throbbing pain
    from splintered shins,
    to chafing thighs
    from where i've been

this, i ask of you,
   to understand from
   where i come, a clue,
   as i sit here, begging
   on my knees, a bruise,
   why don't you walk a mile
   or more in my shoes?

-b.l.g.

substitute

we had to grow up fast
    and take care of ourselves
    because you were
    never there to be our mother

-b.l.g.

family time

normal families bonded over family game nights and fancy dinners in their regal dining rooms with crystal wine glasses.

we bonded over silly things like pulling the 1995 red monte carlo out of the mud under the bridge by the ditch we grew up in and watching dad try to drown my brother in the river after a few beers.

-b.l.g.

the past

the past is not behind me
   it's staring into my soul
   straight ahead, where i can see

a dark cloud rumbling
   sparks of lightning
   illuminating broken
   beer bottles and
   singed spoons

razor blades and
   needles painted red
   band-aids and tissues
   messy sheets on my bed

non-waterproof mascara and
   eyeliner stains on my pillows
   underneath, hidden
   boxes of damp marlboros

muddy shoes crowd
   my sweaty bedside

and a flickering lamp
alerts the life outside
of the unfortunate truth
that i am still alive

the *tick*
   tick
   ticking
   of a clock,
   times moves
   in infinite strides
   with sugar-coated,
   honey-dripped lies
   next to a tea-stained,
   old copy of *the*
   virgin suicides

-b.l.g.

weathered roots

i am from the old house in the ditch
  on the busy highway, where the cars
  honk and the trees sway

i am from the car seat in which I sat, awaiting
  my birth mother as she drowned herself in
  liquor and needles

i am from courtrooms and judges, adoption
  paperwork scattered on the coffee table

i am from crumpled drawings of family trees,
  far too complicated for sketching

i am from Mother to Sister,
  from Grandma to Mom

i am from a broken bicycle in the backyard,
  the wheels still turning

i am from thunderous yelling and crying,
  hurricanes of emotions

i am from tear-stained report cards,
   B's were never welcomed

i am from rough, beige '70s carpet,
   the cigarette smell still lingers

i am from tobacco-infused walls,
   dusty family portraits hanging crooked in the halls

i am from a house turned to home,
   a home turned to Hell

i am from childhood trauma
   and a shattered wishing well

-b.l.g.

white trash

have you ever been
  called white trash?

like cigarette moms
  who smell like ash
  the ones on the porch
  with bras full of cash
  with tattoos on their arms
  and above their ass

like deadbeat dads
  in white wife-beaters
  with a farmer's tan
  as thin as grim reaper
  with hands glued to beer cans
  obvious mouth-breathers

like trailer park fights
  dirt in between our toes
  old, rusty dirt bikes
  and women called hoes
  puddles of spilled pints

upon the garden rows

-b.l.g.

dear grace

do you remember
   when i brushed your hair
   when i gave you piggyback rides
   when i held you when you were scared

do you remember
   the way mama hugged us
   the way mama kissed us
   the way mama loved us

do you remember
   when we were
   together as
   a family

-b.l.g.

mother witch

set the scene in one's home
   whose mother screams
   and claims the throne

dares one enter
   if one is late
   misrepresent her
   and she'll decide your fate

-b.l.g.

dismal land

mama, can we go to disneyland?
  where the grass is green
  and the view is grand?
  maybe one day
  when you return
  my aching pain
  will cease to burn

mama, what have you been up to?
  i have been doing well
  and i really miss you

mama,
  i can't do this anymore
  you don't love me
  and my heart is sore
  you caused this sorrow
  and turned my disneyland
  into dismal land

–b.l.g.

abandon

the crack in the social norm, you abandon
   your baby, crying on the porch
   with no way of understandin'
   and a fire in her chest, scorched

why must you leave, mother?
   what did i do wrong?
   oh, how i miss you, mother
   it has been far too long

is this some cruel punishment?
   i was only an infant, mother
   did i commit such a crime
   that i became a burden or bother?

did i cry too much?
   did i whine and moan
   and put up a big fuss?

how can you believe this
   to be fair, mother?
   a child is supposed bliss,

not some estranged bugger

–b.l.g.

why?

why must you scream
  and terrorize
   my lovely dreams?

you tear apart
  my broken
  heart

i wish you loved me
  the way you claim

-b.l.g.

the last car ride

you were lying in
   the backseat
   wrapped in a blanket,
   looking at me.
   your hazel-brown eyes
   telling me goodbye
   and now all i hold
   at night, is your
   old collar

-b.l.g.

birth

october 14th, 2000
    9:02 am

a poet is born

-b.l.g.

assault

it's hard to put it in words
   the thing that happened to me

judgment—
   it overwhelms me
   but how am i supposed to
   let this go?
   when no one else
   could possibly know?
   or understand

judgment—
   it frightens me
   what could i have done
   when i am no stronger than you
   when i am merely
   a piece of meat

-b.l.g.

little green needles

have you ever wondered
   how similar money is
   to drugs like heroin?

we gotta have it
   gotta have it
   gotta have it

we've become a society
   controlled by a small
   piece of paper

we've become addicted
   like drug abusers

damn, these viridescent bills,
   or should i refer to them as
   little green needles.

   -b.l.g.

guilty

i must have
   flirted too much
   laughed too much
   slurred too much

i must have implied yes
   by my inability
   to say no
   to fight back
   to escape

i must have asked for it
   by smiling at you
   by being neighborly
   by being your friend

i must have worn
   my shorts too short
   and my collar too low
   in my own home
   in my own room
   in my own bed

it must have been
    my fault that you
    got on top of me
    had your way with me
    took my dignity away from me

-b.l.g.

ethanol

why must you drink at all?
   why does it give you tingles
   and euphoria?
   when all it gives me
   is discomfort and fear

last time you drank
   you hit me
   you screamed at me
   you told me i was worthless
   and meant nothing to you

so why do you still drink?
   when you know it hurts
   and makes me think
   that you're a bad parent

-b.l.g.

apparel has no meaning

it doesn't matter what i am wearing
   you will always be staring

that day you bruised me
   that day you used me

i was wearing a black dress
   and black tights

another day,
   i was wearing a sweater
   and blue jeans

no matter what i wore upon my body
   you still seemed to see right through me

today,
   i am wearing a dark hoodie
   and sweats

but you'll just tear those off
   because my clothes are not the problem

you are

–b.l.g.

a little birdie

once there was
   a little birdie
   with dreams to fly

to fly higher
   than anyone else,
   to stand on her own two feet,
   to soar with her own two wings

but with Mama Bird's
   over protection,
   she never knew
   how to recover
   from a fall

-b.l.g.

the old room

dusty shelves hold
  sticky shot glasses
  leftover from the night
  before

worn-out underwire
  bras and hair sheds
  tangled in the carpeted
  floor

crumpled pages fill the
  metal trashcan with
  fast food receipts
  galore

blinking blue lights
  illuminate rusty handles
  on the crooked dresser
  drawer

unopened books
  whisper to you to

dust them off and go
explore

–b.l.g.

incomplete

my body is
   composed of
   delicate puzzle
   pieces,
   all perfectly
   aligned,
   each hole
   fits its knob,
   each tab
   fits its slot

but there's
   a missing piece,
   an empty chunk
   without a key,
   an empty void
   consequently
   incomplete

   -b.l.g.

II

a poet's madness

it will climb into your bed
and crawl inside your head
it will mock the words you said
and tie your lips with thread
it will fill your heart with dread
and make you wish you were dead
–b.l.g.

escape

constant sadness
   dwelling inside of me
   literature and wisdom
   minstrelsy within my soul
   poetry brings comfort
   and ease
   like putting a band-aid
   on a bleeding wound
   or a warm blanket
   on an icy day
   poetry is my hero
   allowing me to escape
   from the monster
   living inside my mind

-b.l.g.

frights

goosebumps
  they cover my entire body
  from head to toe
  chills up my spine

i'm frozen
  can't move

stuck
  like glue

help me
  i'm scared

frightened
  like a deer in headlights

i want to scream
  but i can't

no sound escapes my mouth
  heart beating

loudly in my chest

tears cascading down my face
  my cheeks burn like flames
  sadly,
  i fear myself

–b.l.g.

contemplation

what would happen if people found out
   the reason i care about what they think
   about me?

that i care so much because i know
   that i can be *too much* and
   not enough all at once

that they will realize i am
   broken, unmendable
   unfixable, fragmented,
   and splintered

and they will leave,
   abandon me
   and i will be alone

alone with all of the demons
   inside my head as i
   contemplate over
   using a heavy pistol
   or a razor blade to

escape my exile

-b.l.g.

reliance

things i rely on:

1. ibuprofen to keep the pain away
2. melatonin to help me sleep
3. caffeine to wake me up
4. nicotine to calm my anxiety
5. lexapro to make me happy
6. alcohol to ease my mind
7. weed to explore my imagination

why can't my body do that all on its own?
   why must I rely on these drugs to keep me sane?

-b.l.g.

cluttered

my thoughts surround me like
   this crowded room

with books upon books
   with webs between nooks
   with clothes off hooks

the walls close in,
   soul-crushing from within
   is this how it's always been?

the claustrophobia inside
   keeps me awake at night
   i'm ready to end this fight

sweat pours like rain
   my breath fast with pain
   this must sound insane

but how do i explain
   what's inside my brain?

–b.l.g.

hell flowers

gaze upon the flowers
   swaying in the wind
   their magnificent petals
   plunging
   down
   down
   down
   below life
   underneath
   pure existence
   the conflagration
   incinerating
   the once beautiful rose
   who is now
   just a dead
   weed.

-b.l.g.

detached

after Michael Faudet

you so desire to feel lost,
   erased, like your mind is
   a vacant room, empty, like a
   clear pool of water. how lovely
   to detach from this place
   of uncertainty and hardship, to
   not drown from pressure, to find
   pure lucidity within yourself

-b.l.g.

particles

hand full of pills
   heart full of guilt

watch as my
   particles dissolve
   in a pool of
   your saltwater
   tears

an unequal balance
   within our bond

   -b.l.g.

coward

pop the lid
   pour the pills
   down my throat, they go

cut the skin
   peer within
   so they'll never know

mutilation at its best
   may darkness allow rest

for i cannot unthink
   the tragedy
   they call life

coward, i am
   pathetic
   no good, useless soul

i do not ask for pity
   i simply ask for permission
   to say

goodbye

–b.l.g.

overdose

6:34 pm: my eyelids grow heavy
  6:47 pm: my body slows its pace
  6:58 pm: my chest hurts already
  7:02 pm: i'm ready to leave this place
  7:05 pm: my heart goes steady
  7:22 pm: my head hits the pillowcase
  7:34 pm: i think i took too many
  7:58 pm: i can't even feel my face
  8:02 pm: what if i'm not ready?
  8:29 pm: evidence is gone, i left no trace
  8:42 pm: i took enough, pills aplenty
  8:56 pm: i leave a note i may erase
  9:04 pm: i took more, about twenty
  9:34 pm: i can't escape this headspace
  9:50 pm: i think i took too many
  10:04 pm:

thorn

frankly, i am but a short thorn
   razor-sharp words with rigid might
   why? of course, this way, i was born

narrow eyes, pessimistic scorn
   lie awake late into the night
   frankly, i am but a short thorn

broken my spirit, i shall mourn
   seemingly, no end is in sight
   why? of course, this way, i was born

left fragile pages of mine torn,
   hopeless, from that of which i write
   frankly, i am but a short thorn

with my polished, faux smile adorn
   and all my secrets locked up tight
   why? of course, this way, i was born

however, it's you i must warn
   to desperately calm your fright

frankly, i am but a short thorn
why? of course, this way, i was born

-b.l.g.

outside perspective

i wanna watch
   my cold, shivering body in the dark

i wanna see
   my eyes lose their color and spark

i wanna behold
   the moment i bleed gold

i wanna spy
   as i take the blade into my hand
   and say goodbye

–b.l.g.

routine

face routine:

1. wet the skin with warm water
2. apply face wash and scrub softly
3. rinse face
4. peer into your sunken eyes
5. ask if you should keep going
6. contemplate different ways to cope
7. glance down at your body (cringe in disgust)
8. add vitamin c serum to dry areas
9. add witch hazel toner
10. don't forget to moisturize!

-b.l.g.

reflection of insanity

watch closely
    as the numbness begins to set in
    the emptiness in her soul
    the pain and despair in her eyes
    the vacancy in her heart

she is gone
    never to come back the same
    locked up
    all alone in solitude

i look into the reflection
    only to see
    the girl with
    the swollen eyes
    the trampled heart
    the corrupted mind
    is me.

-b.l.g.

stickers

the beeping of the heart monitor and nurses' hushed voices
from the hall awaken me. as i look around the room, i can
remember from last time—they are about to move me upstairs
to the pavilion soon. the young nurse comes in with a smile on
her sun-kissed face. *hi, sweetie. can you stand up for me?* i stand.
great. now, i'm going to put some stickers on you, is that okay? i
nod. she begins to stick me with ice-cold electrodes scattered
across my skin. goosebumps rise up on my arms and legs. *i'm
sorry, sweetie. i know it's cold.* she begins to insert wires into the
stickers as if i am a robot—as if i am a science experiment.

-b.l.g.

the truth behind dreams

dreams?
   more like nightmares
   eating at your soul
   ripping your heart out
   dragging your corpse to hell
   making you wish for things
   you cannot have
   creating a moment
   or memory
   you will never be able to regain
   hurting you
   emotionally
   leaving you breathless
   and scarred
   permanently

-b.l.g.

sweet sedative

it is an august afternoon.
   shoes squeak on the tacky tiles
   i should've known back in june
   that i'd eventually return
   to this solemn exile so soon,
   to be trapped here in this
   godforsaken white room.

the yellow socks on my feet
   alert the staff i am high risk
   so i lay waiting for my treat
   in this bed of itchy cloth,
   my pills; however, not sweet,
   i await my miniature dessert
   to take my cherished sleep

  -b.l.g.

plague

when asked the question,
   how often do you think about suicide?
   i usually lie and say,
   only for a split second...

however, one second turns
   into one minute
   one minute turns
   into one hour
   one hour turns
   into a whole day

but the whole day
   turns into a week
   and by then,
   i am long gone.

it is not a serious plan
   it is merely an invasion of my mind,
   a plague on my brain that i
   cannot find the cure for,
   no matter how many pills i take,

trying to suffocate the sounds of the voices
telling me that i am not enough for this world.

-b.l.g.

one day

one day
  my thighs
  will say goodbye
  to each other

one day
  my collar bones
  will peek through
  and say hello

one day
  the gap in my teeth
  and the dimple
  in my chin
  will disappear

one day
  i will look into
  the mirror
  and love what
  i see.

–b.l.g.

social anxiety

sweet, sweet silence
   drifting away from me,
   like receding waves
   on a shore,
   leaving me shaking
   and restless.

pardon me, sir.
   excuse me, ma'am.

i am but a burden
   upon all living creatures,
   bothering all life
   with my existence.

leave me in my corner
   with my haunted thoughts
   and impulsive ideas,
   wishes to be or not to be
   perceived

perhaps,

the unperceived silence
is as calming as subtle waves

so please,
do not speak or else,
my sweet, sweet silence
will leave me.

–b.l.g.

fall

sugar skulls
   candy souls
    scent of pumpkin spice
    chilly nights
    vampire bites
    dying would be nice

-b.l.g.

overdue

help me
   help me stop bleeding
   the monster is taking control
   he's killing me inside
   make it stop
   hurry

time is ticking

  -b.l.g.

vices

one more shot
   one more hit
   maybe then
   i'll give a shit

about myself,
   about the world
   my mind open
   my heart unfurled

–b.l.g.

ethanol II

why must i drink at all?
  why does it give me tingles
  and euphoria?
  when all it really gives me
  is a throat aflame,
  regrets and shame?

but who am i to blame?
  when it's all i've learned
  from a young age
  to numb the pain
  with a drink

the sound of a *clink!*
  throwing back shots
  so i don't have to think

–b.l.g.

smolder

i am nothing more but a wilting carnation
   my petals falling upon the ground
   appearing far too gone from salvation
   my stem aflame, a sight so profound!

-b.l.g.

tired

i cannot fathom this existence any longer
   i am merely tired and weak
   they say pain only makes you stronger
   but i am too exhausted to speak

-b.l.g.

racing

my thoughts race like greyhounds on a track
    faster and faster and faster
    from overwhelming pressure, my body starts to crack
    until there is nothing left for me to give

-b.l.g.

the girl in the mirror

we talk often
   about nothing in
   particular
   how was your day?
   —oh, it was fine, thanks.

but sometimes,
   we play the blame
   game on each other

this is all your fault
   why won't you just
   listen to me?

—why are you so
   reckless, so stubborn
   so hideously toxic
   you make it so hard
   to breathe.

we are not friends.

–b.l.g.

breakfast

sometimes, nothing is
   more beautiful than the
   rays of sun peering in over
   your bed from the window,
   the smoke dancing in
   the sunlight

   –b.l.g.

alone

cold and empty
   windy and chilly
   ahh!
   the little girl screams
   as she falls
   down a hill
   nobody finds her
   nobody cares
   she's all alone
   drenched in blood
   covered in cuts
   for hours
   she cries
   until
   BANG!
   she dies.

  –b.l.g.

maybe

pain
   it's better than nothing
   better than feeling like a ghost
   gone
   forever
   maybe it's the easy way out
   maybe it's not

   –b.l.g.

pain

pain

you haven't felt real pain
    until you've looked up to the sky
    screaming, *why, God, why?*
    and *i wanna die*

no one gets it because
    it's all just *in your brain*
    no one gets it because
    they haven't felt real pain

–b.l.g.

clichés

clichés

sitting here
   drinking a mug of hot tea
   waiting for you
   to think of me

i don't know
   where i'd go
   if you left
   and crushed my soul

it pains me
   to realize
   you could leave
   at any moment

but this is all
   just some cliché
   and *it'll get better*
   because that's what they say
   to those with problems

to those who aren't okay

–b.l.g.

if only

if only

if only you knew
   how bad it really is

how badly i crave the
   feeling of my skin on fire
   from the heat of
   a bloody blade
   clutched by
   my own hand

how badly i desire the
   feeling of the dark
   red liquid cascading
   down my thigh,
   tracing the curve
   of my knee

how badly i wish
   these feelings would
   end

–b.l.g.

III

a poet's love

my love is a warm glow
like a summer's day
wrapping him in a blanket
much more temperate
than the Sun, herself
-b.l.g.

sweet stranger

sweet stranger,
  i haven't known for long

sweet stranger,
  with you is where i belong

-b.l.g.

march

the day i met you,
   nerves shot down
   my spine
   pins and needles pricked
   my fingers
   flames engulfed
   my cheeks

the day we kissed,
   you broke down
   my walls
   you filled the hole in
   my heart
   you held me and taught me

it's okay to love again

–b.l.g.

dog tags

gleaming silver
   dangling from your neck
   a kiss
   a peck
   trailing down your chest
   ice cold metal
   sends chills down my spine

your last name,
   a name we'll soon share,
   engraved into shiny steel,
   that night
   i knew you were mine

  -b.l.g.

miles

over a thousand miles away
   why must you be so far?
   i miss those days
   singing in my car
   at the top of our lungs

i'll always remember
   the songs we sung
   the look in your eyes
   the breath off your tongue

–b.l.g.

sandy kisses

and as we both lie here
   the stars reflect on your teeth
   with the waves crashing near
   sprinkled sand on the blanket beneath
   with sea grass and water so clear
   this is where we choose to meet

where shore greets damp sand
   newborn turtles flee past
   you reach for my small hand
   and my heart's beating fast

  –b.l.g.

affinity

affectionate lover, i'm so
   fond of your lips,
   forever plump and
   inviting to kiss.
   nighttime drives and
   indigo skies. i can
   tell one day i'll be
   yours and you, mine.

   -b.l.g.

sheets

shiny silk
   caresses our bodies
   as endless euphoria
   fills our brains
   and heavy kisses
   preoccupy our mouths

-b.l.g.

stars

i look over to you in the night,

— *what are you doing?*

i'm tracing the stars

-b.l.g.

fate

for you, i
   am infatuated,
   truly mesmerized
   entirely

how did you know
   i needed you most?

-b.l.g.

bookstore

let me take you to
   the bookstore and
   sit in a corner with
   my head on your
   shoulder, listening
   to you breathe as
   we both indulge
   ourselves in the
   pages of our
   own love story

   -b.l.g.

attraction

affectionate lover, i'm so
   tempted to stay, locked
   tight in your arms,
   romanticizing you
   as young artists do,
   capturing the light
   till dawn turns to night
   inside sweet dreams of
   ours on this brisk, winter
   night.

-b.l.g.

head to toe

your head
  your eyes
  your ears
  your nose
  your lips
  your kiss
  your jaw
  your soul
  your neck
  your chest
  your heart
  your love
  your sex
  your body
  your thighs
  your calves
  your ankles
  your toes

beg to be mine!

–b.l.g.

suddenly

we are laying here
   the lights dim

and suddenly
   i'm not thinking of him

i'm thinking of something sweeter
   something more rich
   suddenly
   my feelings begin to switch

no longer am i broken
   no longer am i empty
   suddenly
   your eyes begin to tempt me

we are laying here
   everything feels new

and suddenly
   i'm thinking of you

–b.l.g.

situationship

why are we trapped
   in this purgatory of
   a situationship

all because your
   scared of committing
   to a relationship

but you have me
   and i have you
   so why are we
   stuck in this room
   of confusion

vacant vicinity
   of limbo before
   we eventually call
   it quits and you split

why don't we just
   slap a label on it?

-b.l.g.

autumn

you feel like
    a nap at 2 pm on
    an autumn afternoon
    the drizzling rain
    singing a lullaby
    with a pumpkin
    scented candle
    keeping me warm

  -b.l.g.

three words

they live on the tip of my tongue
   these pesky three words
   i can't say because we're too young
   it'll be easier if they're slurred
   an intoxicated song sung

maybe i'll let my eyes tell you
   let them serenade you with
   the ocean waves of tears
   passionate lullabies late
   at night inside your room

-b.l.g.

IV

a poet's heartbreak

you said i would be
the one to leave
but you're the one
walking out the door
–b.l.g.

left for dead

as i write your name,
   my pencil sheds lead
   from gripping the wood
   so hard, my knuckles turn red

you left me alone
   with demons in my head
   all on my own
   you left me for dead

now all i can do
   is write what you said
   over and over, you
   soiled our bed

you left me alone
   and burned every thread
   all on my own
   you left me for dead

  -b.l.g.

to my ex-lover

does my name taste
  so good
  that after all these years
  it stills rolls off
  your tongue

-b.l.g.

home

you were my home
   from every tile
   in my kitchen
   to every book
   on my shelf

but i was just
   your doormat

-b.l.g.

bitter

look at you with
   your glass of cabernet
   tasting of black
   cherry and disarray

-b.l.g.

corrupt

falling in love with you
   was like lighting a fresh
   cigarette,
   it's tightly wrapped paper
   not yet corrupted by the
   fire

until we flipped the
   switch on our gold-plated
   zippo, igniting the flames
   and burning the crisp
   filter

taking long drags of
   the tube of toxicity,
   filling our lungs with
   the addicting fumes

  -b.l.g.

cut

you told me
   you were leaving
   and it felt like a
   razor blade
   slicing into my skin,
   the icy burn stinging
   as the blood cascaded
   like the tears i shed
   for you

you cut me deep

-b.l.g.

beg

i can't make you love me
   no matter how hard i try
   to make you feel what i feel
   no matter how hard i cry

-b.l.g.

trust

trusting you was
   regretful, an
   unfortunate
   spell you cast to
   trick me into staying

-b.l.g.

leech

i'm a pessimistic parasite
   sucking the blood
   from your soft skin

following you everywhere
   you go and every place
   that you've been

you can't get rid of me
   pull me off, i dare you
   can't you see?
   unfortunately for you,
   you're nothing without me

try to shake me off
   i'll stay latched on
   like handcuffs in the dark
   or tight ropes you don

i'll do anything for you
   suck the poison from your veins
   just give me a chance or two

i'll drink your blood as it drains

i'll leave hickeys on your skin
   marking my sacred territory
   you'll know where i've been
   my intentions predatory

don't throw me away
   'cause you know
   i'll always stay
   to suck out your soul
   as a form of foreplay

-b.l.g.

ode to the prince

cheers to the prince, you are! how inspiring,
   my darling love. you inspire me to write
   romantic poetry, how admiring,
    dozens of sonnets stem from summer nights

but, my love, when the cool wind gets cooler
   and the leaves begin to fall from the trees
   you twist my arm, you wretched abuser
   i beg for your love on my hands and knees

why must you lie to me for all these years?
   breaking my poor heart little by little
   shredding my hope, proving truth to my fears
   such deceit, you played me like a fiddle

you fabricated your love, stole my crown
   i should have always known you'd let me down

-b.l.g.

seasons

you come and go
  like the seasons
  so many different shades
  of different colors.
  such a beautiful palette

i miss summer most of all
  your hands are the sun
  that warms my whole body
  you graze my skin with your light

i dread the time of winter
  when you're cold and distant
  and your beautiful green leaves
  fall to the ground
  leaving your branches bare
  and unrecognizable

leaving me shivering
  alone in the dark

-b.l.g.

what about me?

can't you see
   i cannot breathe
   without the help
   of your precious lungs
   and your sweet air
   filling my chest with
   love and care

-b.l.g.

june 24th, 2020

the day that time travel was invented

-b.l.g.

to my ex-lover II

how bad do you miss me?
  because her name
  also starts with "B'
  and she kind of looks like me

blonde hair
  blue eyes
  tan skin
  how nice

how bad do you miss me?
  because she's just another
  version of me
  to keep you company
  so when i'm gone,
  you won't be so lonely.

 -b.l.g.

the letter "N"

this haunted letter
   i dread so much
   could kill me so easily
   with a smile and a touch
   your name will be burned
   into my skin
   into my veins
   into my brain

please get out!
   i curse your name

-b.l.g.

nicotine and heartbreak

a puff of smoke
   escaping my lungs
   how can i understand
   when you speak in tongues
   in rhymes
   in riddles
   you make me feel good
   initially,
   high
   buzzed
   as time goes on,
   it gets harder to breathe
   a cough
   a wheeze
   why can't i leave
   your memory
   your face
   your taste?

you're like a bad addiction

  -b.l.g.

decaying

my eyelids purple
  my lips blue
  who am i
  without you

-b.l.g.

malibu nights

i saw that you were with
   her at 3am alone
   and you wouldn't
   even answer your phone
   what was i supposed to think?
   i guess i should have known
   that you two were meant to be

but instead, i flicked
   off the cap of malibu
   and thought only of
   memories, me and you
   drowned myself in tears
   and coconut rum, too

a knock on the door
   he invited himself in
   climbed onto my bed
   took ahold of my chin
   kiss me, said he
   drunken kisses begin
   unease on my end

he committed a sin

help, i wanted to shout
   through my intoxication
   the words wouldn't come out
   he blatantly ignored my
   discomfort and doubt

the next morning,
   i woke up lost
   in a mess of sheets
   fingers crossed
   that it was a dream
   that he was gone

but he wasn't gone
   and it wasn't a dream
   next to me, a yawn
   from the mouth
   that kissed upon
   my unconsenting lips

to make matters worse,
   i texted my so-called
   friends, conversed
   about my late night
   scandals, how perverse,
   she told you a story
   she must've rehearsed

you called me later

screaming into my ear
about my recent affair
after all these years
but we weren't together
and you wouldn't hear
my excuses, my answers

you claimed i was a cheat
but how is that fair?
i was incapacitated
you weren't even there
you hurt me badly
but you don't care

you won't accept i was raped
because you never cared
it hurt your fragile ego
because i was shared

-b.l.g.

space

once there was a time
  when we could collide
  my atoms, yours
  your atoms, mine

but now, it feels as if
  tsunamis of stars, a
  plethora of planets
  divide us, distantly

with nuclear fission,
  you were on a mission
  to shoot your neutrons,
  into my nucleus,
  splitting our atomic
  union

our cosmic
  entanglement
  tangled no longer

-b.l.g.

lost

the day i lost you
i lost me, too

–b.l.g.

blocked

you blow up my phone
   even though i'm not home
   you say you shoulda known
   that i'd leave you alone

but, baby, you broke me
   with all the toxicity
   drunk off your melodies
   ignoring the remedies

you call me again
   wondering where i've been
   assume i slept with him
   committing a sin

but, baby, that's not fair
   'cause this love is rare
   we were a good pair
   'till you didn't care

you drew the line
   and wasted my time

i thought we were fine
shoulda seen the signs

but, baby, it's time to go
   don't call my phone
   just drive on home
   just fucking leave me alone

–b.l.g.

party foul

my heart is a shot glass
   delicate and fragile
   drowning in a brass-
   colored liquor downed
   by college frat guys
   at parties in filthy
   fraternity mansions
   with sticky wooden floors
   and used shirts and bras
   hanging on knobs of doors
   with thick air smelling of
   skunk, sweat, and sex,
   the smell of desperation
   mixed with anxious
   alcoholic motivation
   ignoring the consequences
   of inevitable damnation
   blending their gin with sin

until it's 2am and
   the cops bust in
   and the sweaty hand

of a sweaty man
knocks over my glass
spilling its sticky substance
and shattering into fragments
on the sticky wooden floors
erasing its existence

–b.l.g.

fallacious conclusions

i sit quietly alone
  and sip my sweet tea
  drip
  drip
  drip
  the sound of rain
  against the tin roof
  i ponder through
  past memories
  i remember the days
  when i thought i would never
  make it this far
  when i thought you would never
  leave me
  when i thought i would never
  regain my strength
  and move on

-b.l.g.

time flies

four years
   forty-eight months
   two hundred nine weeks
   one thousand sixty days
   thirty-five thousand forty hours

all that time
   we spent together

all for nothing

-b.l.g.

"best friend"

thirteen years
   down the drain
   i was there
   through all the pain

but where are you now?

-b.l.g.

ode to the prince II

my cruel prince, you inspire me to write
  how i love the way you hurt, lie and fight,
  invading my mind day and through the night,
  daydreaming about a dress made in white

let me compare you to a fallen arch
  you are more toxic, shrieval and evil
  bold clouds dull the fateful flowers of march,
  but springtime cannot contain your needle

your hatred dissects my body in ways,
  cuts me deeper every day, pricks my heart
  and lets it bleed, longing for me to stay
  you paint with my blood—your sick, twisted art

now i must stay away, get a fresh start
  remember my cool words whilst we're apart

-b.l.g.

137

goodbye

i remember the day you left
   february fifth

screaming and crying
   the taste of salty tears on my tongue
   the neighbors heard it all

on my hands and knees
   begging you "please,
   don't go."

–b.l.g.

one night stand

maybe i can hide my pain
   while sleeping with another
   feeling their skin on mine
   burying my sorrow
   in a pillow
   and messy sheets
   drunken kisses
   and sweet treats

maybe i can forget the
   heartbreak you caused,
   the splinters on my fingertips
   from the shattered pieces
   of my heart

maybe i can forget you

– b.l.g.

V

a poet's recovery

i've spent many years
seeing the glass
as half empty
but i'm ready to find
the potential
of my glass half full
–b.l.g.

reflection

since we've been apart
   i've learned
   you're not a work of art
   i've learned
   you don't possess a spark
   i've learned
   you don't have a heart

i was in love with
   the idea of you
   i created a perfect,
   polished version of you
   i fell in love with the love
   i gave to you

i fell in love with myself

  -b.l.g.

postpartum

i will never be
   your perfect housewife
   all dolled up for you
   with a hot and ready stew
   with our quintessential life

you don't know what it's like
   screaming like a banshee on
   the inside, to be trapped here
   to be forced into this frontier
   taking care of your spawn

-b.l.g.

the artist

i am an artist,
   sketching and drawing
   different versions of
   you

using my charcoal vines
   and pencils to blend
   every piece together

perfecting your portrait
   creating my flawless
   partner, my angel

i believed i had
   drawn you well

but it was all a fantasy
   it was all me

i invented you

–b.l.g.

healing

healing from you
  is like having a
  broken rib
  no one can see it
  but it hurts to
  breathe

-b.l.g.

my universe

you were your own sun
   revolving around yourself
   and you were my world

but i've realized i was
   out of orbit

-b.l.g.

perfect match

now, the only use
   for these pictures of you
   is to light my cigarette
   with their flame

what a perfect match

–b.l.g.

generosity

i caught myself doing it again,
   giving a man my time and energy
   before he proves himself to be worth it
   giving a man my love and affection
   before he has earned it

mirror

after all these years
  being scared to look
  into the mirror at
  myself

i decided i am going
  to love that girl
  reflecting back at
  me with all the
  love that you
  ignored

-b.l.g.

self-love

i've realized that
   i can't make you
   love me

i can only
   love myself

-b.l.g.

resilience

remember when you
  eventually
  said that
  i would
  languish
  in my despair?
  even looking at me
  now, you
  can see that i've
  elevated myself

without you

-b.l.g.

poetic pleasure

we were just a bunch of horny poets
　　searching for anything to inspire us
　　reaching for our vices at our lowest
　　killing our minds and bodies without fuss

rifling through pages and pages of books
　　but the stories of others in despair
　　won't save us from the tight rope and strong hooks
　　depressing, isn't it? i know it's not fair

but what do we do with this parasite,
　　this leech sucking our soul from our weak minds
　　when we're compelled to kiss late at night
　　looking for our own slice of paradise

we were just a bunch of horny poets
　　making love in the verses of sonnets

　-b.l.g.

false expectations

our relationship
  ending used to be
  my nightmare

but upon closer
  inspection, it
  became my
  dream

–b.l.g.

relapse

it comes in
  again like
  the clouds
  of smoke,
  their milky
  white spirals
  spilling out
  of my lungs
  every now
  and then

 -b.l.g.

ash

sometimes my chest
   disintegrates, crumbling
   into peppered bits

but sometimes,
   i pick myself up
   and blow the
   ash off into the
   freeing air

-b.l.g.

i am

a poet
  a scholar
  an artist
  a singer
  a dancer
  a teacher
  a dreamer

don't take away my life
  because you think
  you have the right

my body, my choice

-b.l.g.

burned

i'm tired of
   lighting myself
   on fire just
   to keep
   you warm

–b.l.g.

for gage

your life is just as paramount
   as any sacred text

each day, a page
   each season, a chapter

you might reach the point
   where you find yourself
   reading one of those
   sad, heart-shattering sections

and it's so depressing
   you want to put down the book
   and end it before you finish

but what you don't know
   is that the chapter after the bad one
   has the potential of being the best
   in the whole novel

don't get discouraged
   finish your book

–b.l.g.

little star

how are the moon,
   the sun, and
   all their subjects?

can you see jupiter
   and venus,
   mars, and
   saturn?

are you finally
   at rest from
   all of the pain
   inside your chest?

-b.l.g.

i wish i knew

you were falling apart
   and i had no clue
   the pain in your heart
   only grew and grew

little sprout, you
   were too young
   i wish you knew
   you weren't done

there's too much
   good life to live,
   hearts to touch
   good love to give

i wish i knew
   before it was
   too late

-b.l.g.

little brother

it wasn't supposed to end this way. you were supposed to live longer than me, by years upon years. you had so much life to live, little star. you had so many dreams, little sprout—so many dreams that you won't be able to accomplish.

-b.l.g.

resting sunshine

yawn, the sun goes
   goodnight, my sweet
   says the moon
   farewell, my love
   we will meet again soon
   i shall wrap you in clouds
   all cozy and soft
   dream sweet dreams
   think lyrical thoughts
   take your special place
   high in my heart
   rest, my dear
   because even the most
   beautiful works of art
   need to unwind

-b.l.g.

runaway

i want to run away
   into the woods
   alone, leave everyone
   behind to live with
   the moss and the
   mushrooms

-b.l.g.

dear younger self

i am sorry for all that
   you have been through,
   for all that pain you
   have felt, that burning
   in your chest when someone
   approaches you, when someone
   asks you a question, when
   someone demands an answer.

i am sorry that you feel the need
   to end your life from all of the
   heartache others have
   unforgivably caused you.

their actions do not define you

-b.l.g.

you belong

believe in your
   earthly spirit to be
   loved in every form
   of you, every shape of
   natural beauty
   growing in bloom

-b.l.g.

her

small, quiet, mouse-like
   friend to the shy, sister to the broken
   looked up to the sky
   with words soft-spoken
   who loved the waves
   who loved the ocean
   feelings of self-hatred, guilt, and abandonment
   fears of solitude, judgment, and enclosurement
   who composed sweet melodies with her words
   who desired change in herself and the world
   born an accident, living on purpose

-b.l.g.

About the Author

Brooke L. Gardner (aka b.l.g.) is a poet, writer, and author of the collection of poetry, *Tea Stains & Cigarettes.* Brooke earned a BA in creative writing from the University of West Florida in 2022. Brooke's passion for writing began when she was in elementary school, writing short stories on scraps of notebook paper. In middle school, Brooke discovered the art of poetry through works from Edgar Allan Poe and Langston Hughes. Originally, Brooke began writing poetry as a means to cope with depression and anxiety. Now, she hopes that people who read her work will find comfort in knowing they are not alone with the demons of mental health problems.

You can connect with me on:
- 🌐 https://brookegardner.journoportfolio.com
- 🔗 https://www.instagram.com/sincerely.blg

Made in the USA
Columbia, SC
21 December 2022

74738573R00112